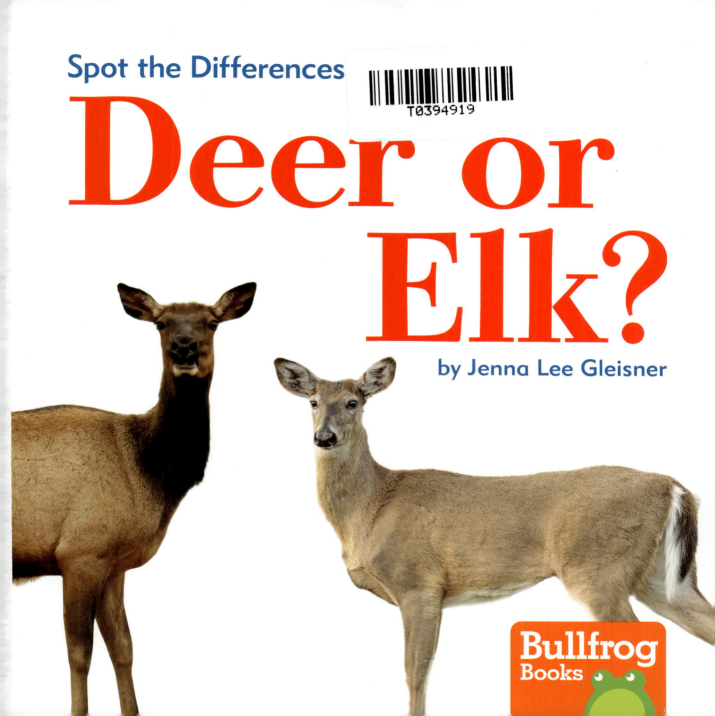

Spot the Differences

Deer or Elk?

by Jenna Lee Gleisner

Bullfrog Books

Ideas for Parents and Teachers

Bullfrog Books let children practice reading informational text at the earliest reading levels. Repetition, familiar words, and photo labels support early readers.

Before Reading

- Discuss the cover photo. What does it tell them?

- Look at the picture glossary together. Read and discuss the words.

Read the Book

- "Walk" through the book and look at the photos. Let the child ask questions. Point out the photo labels.

- Read the book to the child, or have them read independently.

After Reading

- Prompt the child to think more. Ask: Have you ever seen a deer or elk? Would you like to?

Bullfrog Books are published by Jump!
5357 Penn Avenue South
Minneapolis, MN 55419
www.jumplibrary.com

Copyright © 2025 Jump! International copyright reserved in all countries. No part of this book may be reproduced in any form without written permission from the publisher.

Library of Congress Cataloging-in-Publication Data

Names: Gleisner, Jenna Lee, author.
Title: Deer or elk? / by Jenna Lee Gleisner.
Description: Minneapolis, MN: Jump!, Inc., [2025]
Series: Spot the differences | Includes index.
Audience: Ages 5–8
Identifiers: LCCN 2024023379 (print)
LCCN 2024023380 (ebook)
ISBN 9798892136785 (hardcover)
ISBN 9798892136792 (paperback)
ISBN 9798892136808 (ebook)
Subjects: LCSH: Deer—Juvenile literature.
Elk—Juvenile literature.
Classification: LCC QL737.U55 G58 2025 (print)
LCC QL737.U55 (ebook)
DDC 599.65—dc23/eng/20240621
LC record available at https://lccn.loc.gov/2024023379
LC ebook record available at https://lccn.loc.gov/2024023380

Editor: Katie Chanez
Designer: Emma Almgren-Bersie

Photo Credits: photographybyJHWilliams/iStock, cover (deer); Robert Harding Video/Shutterstock, cover (elk); Cannon Colegrove/Shutterstock, 1 (left); JoanneStrell/Shutterstock, 1 (right); Tom Reichner/Shutterstock, 3, 8–9, 23tl; Wirestock/iStock, 4; Harry Collins Photography/Shutterstock, 5; efenzi/iStock, 6–7 (top); Iv-olga/Shutterstock, 6–7 (bottom); Nnehring/iStock, 10–11, 23bm; Jeffrey B. Banke/Shutterstock, 12–13; Natural History Archive/Alamy, 14–15, 23br; Donna Feledichuk/iStock, 16–17; Pat & Chuck Blackley/Alamy, 18–19, 23tm, 23tr; Carol Hamilton/iStock, 20 (deer); Kristine Rad/Shutterstock, 20 (track); Mumemories/Shutterstock, 21 (elk); Max Allen/Alamy, 21 (track); Dennis W Donohue/Shutterstock, 22 (left); MattCuda/iStock, 22 (right); epantha/iStock, 23bl; meunierd/Shutterstock, 24 (top); Photo Focus Photography/Shutterstock, 24 (bottom).

Printed in the United States of America at Corporate Graphics in North Mankato, Minnesota.

Table of Contents

Antlers and Hooves	4
See and Compare	20
Quick Facts	22
Picture Glossary	23
Index	24
To Learn More	24

How to Use This Book

In this book, you will see pictures of both deer and elk. Can you tell which one is in each picture?

Hint: You can find the answers if you flip the book upside down!

Antlers and Hooves

This is a deer.

This is an elk.

They look alike.
But they are different.
How?
Let's see!

Males have antlers.
An elk's point back.
A deer's point to the front.
Which is this?

Answer: deer

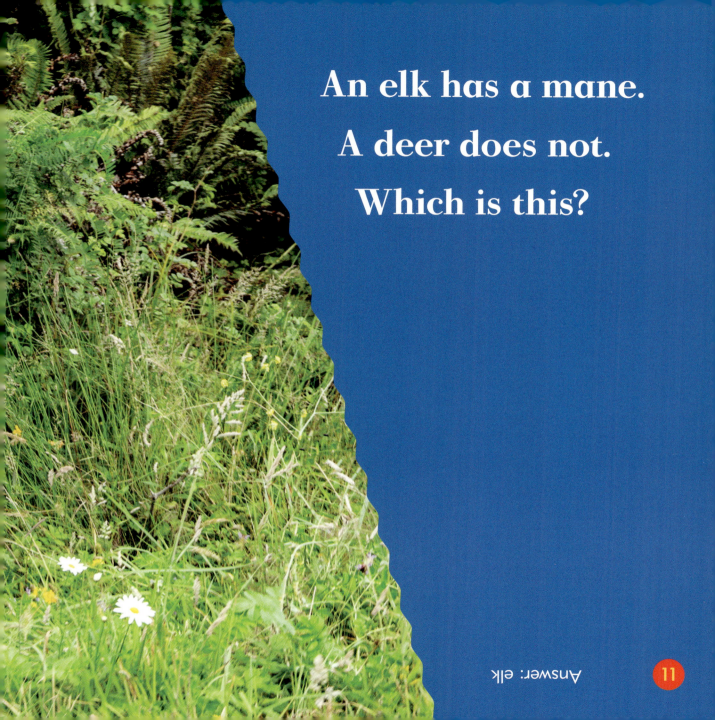

An elk has a mane.
A deer does not.
Which is this?

Answer: elk

An elk has a short tail.
A deer's is longer.
Which is this?

Answer: deer

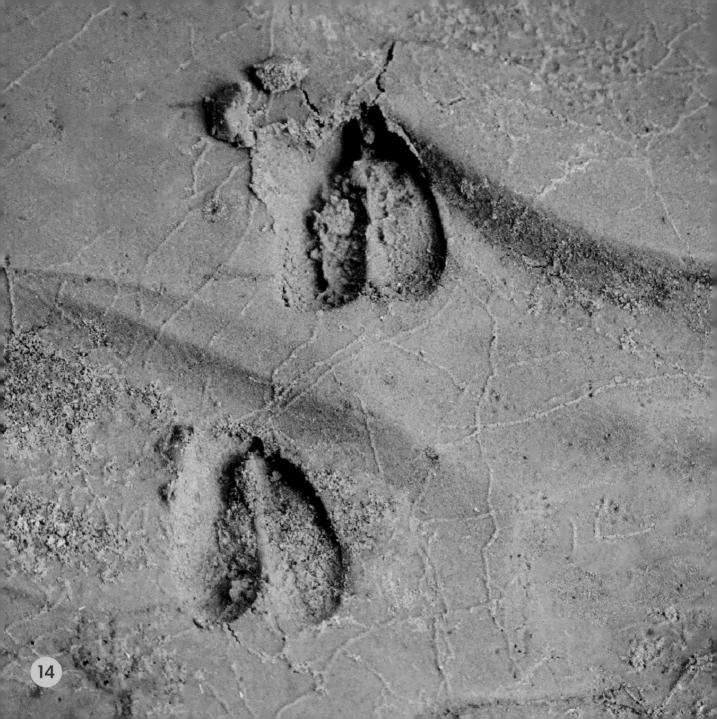

Both have hooves.

A deer's are shaped like hearts.

An elk's are round.

Whose tracks are these?

Answer: deer

A male elk calls.
It is loud.
A male deer does not.
Which is this?

Answer: elk

Both graze.
Elk graze in big herds.
Deer do not.
Which are these?

Answer: elk

See and Compare

Deer

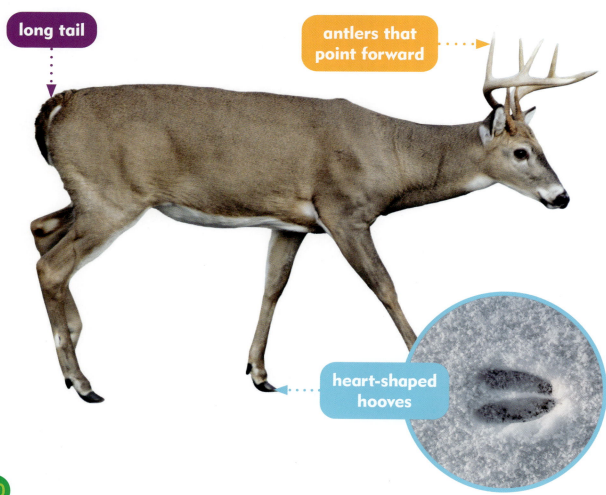

long tail

antlers that point forward

heart-shaped hooves

20

Elk

- small, short tail
- antlers that point back
- mane
- round hooves

21

Quick Facts

Deer and elk are similar. But they have some differences. Take a look!

Deer

- about 3 feet (0.9 meters) tall at shoulder
- weigh up to 450 pounds (204 kilograms)
- males make soft grunting noises

Elk

- about 5 feet (1.5 m) tall at shoulder
- weigh up to 1,000 pounds (454 kg)
- males make a loud call called a bugle

Picture Glossary

antlers
Large bony structures on a deer, elk, or moose head.

graze
To feed on grass.

herds
Large groups of animals that stay together.

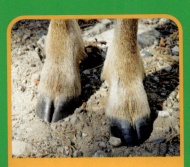

hooves
The hard feet of deer and elk.

mane
Long, thick hair on the neck of an animal.

tracks
Marks that a moving animal leaves behind.

Index

antlers 8
calls 16
graze 19
herds 19
hooves 15
males 8, 16
mane 11
point 8
tail 12
tracks 15

To Learn More

Finding more information is as easy as 1, 2, 3.
❶ Go to www.factsurfer.com
❷ Enter "deerorelk?" into the search box.
❸ Choose your book to see a list of websites.